MW01138627

Tales of Wizardly Whimsy
By Jeffrey Schweitzer

Bindlestick
Books

Santa Fe, New Mexico

Published by
Bindlestick Books
616 1/2 Canyon Road, Unit A
Santa Fe, NM 87501
www.bindlestickbooks.com

Special Edition
ISBN 978-0-692-70929-0

Printed in The United States of America

There are tales of the Wizard who lived in the sky,
He mostly kept to himself and was really quite shy.

The Wizard was ancient all the legends would say,
Most agreed he was three thousand years and just one day.

It seemed he was only ever seen from a great distance,
Which had created some skepticism about his existence.

He was often reported wandering the forest at night,
Seeking ingredients for his spells amid the moonlight.

It's believed that an old crow followed him wherever he went,
Causing him considerable annoyance and endless torment.

It's said the passages below his castle formed an elaborate maze,
And anyone who ventured inside would be lost for days.

The locals believed he was truly blessed,
Because butterflies surrounded him when he stopped to rest.

Some said the trees spoke to him when they rustled their leaves,
But this was a tale that almost no one believed.

It's believed when he traveled that a fog would always follow,
But investigating this claim had proven quite hollow.

People claimed to have seen him high in the hills,
Showing off an impressive array of wizardly skills.

One spring morning someone claimed to have seen,
The Wizard breathing clouds into the sky as if it routine.

It's believed that he created a hot air balloon just for a laugh,
Crafted from scraps of old clothes and the heat from his staff.

Late one evening a villager proclaimed in shock,
That he had seen the Wizard taking the moon for a walk.

People believed that he rode a giant magic turtle everywhere,
Up and down, all around and from here to there.

Some people claimed he displayed a unique flair
For making things appear from out of thin air.

Old legends about him seem to persist,
And there are some who think that he may still exist.

But if he's still out there we surely would know,
Because the tales of his wizardly whimsy would certainly grow.